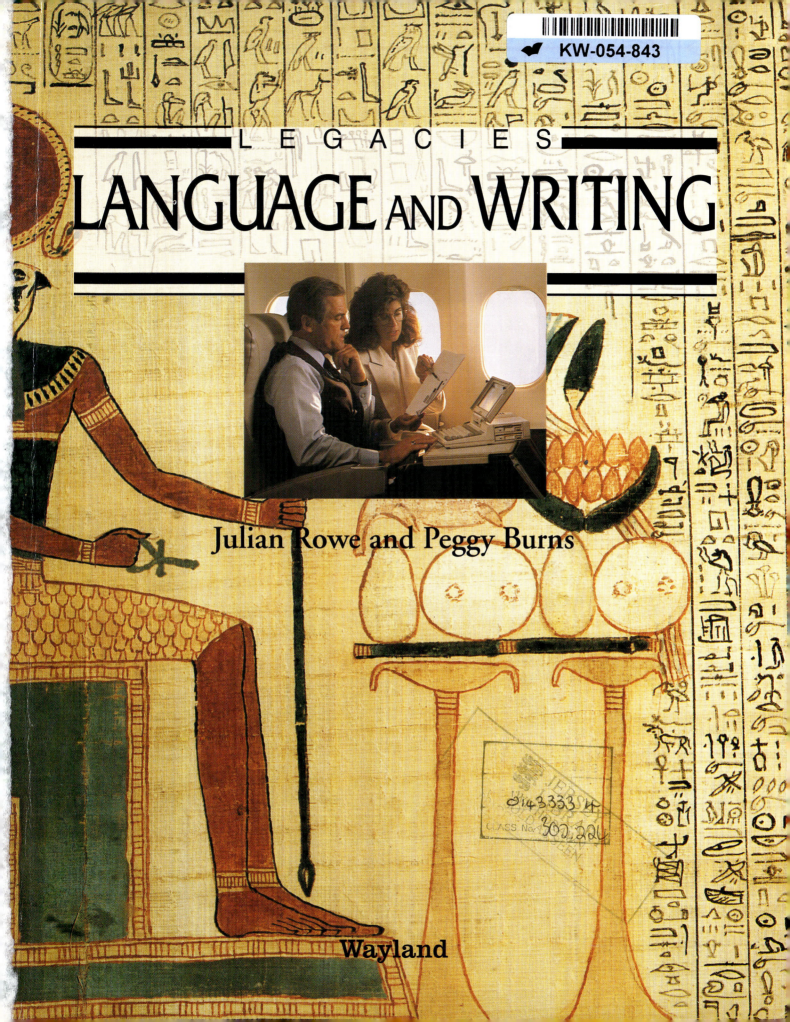

LEGACIES

LANGUAGE AND WRITING

Julian Rowe and Peggy Burns

Wayland

Legacies

Architecture
Costume and Clothes
Language and Writing
Politics and Government
Science and Technology
Sports and Entertainment

Cover pictures: 5,000 years ago, the ancient Egyptians kept records by writing hieroglyphs on papyrus. Today's busy executives keep their records on laptop computers.

Series editor: Polly Goodman
Editorial management: Serpentine Editorial
Series designer: Liz Miller
Book designer: Malcolm Walker

First published in 1995 by
Wayland (Publishers) Limited
61 Western Road, Hove
East Sussex BN3 1JD, England

© Copyright 1995 Wayland (Publishers) Limited

British Library Cataloguing in Publication Data
  Burns, Peggy
  Language and Writing. – (Legacies Series)
  I. Title II. Series
  410.9

ISBN 0 7502 1271 3

Typeset by Kudos Editorial and Design Services
Printed and bound in Italy by G.Canale & C.S.p.A., Turin

Contents

Legacies are things that are handed down from an ancestor or predecessor. The modern world has inherited many different legacies from ancient civilizations. This book explores the legacies of language and writing from the ancient world.

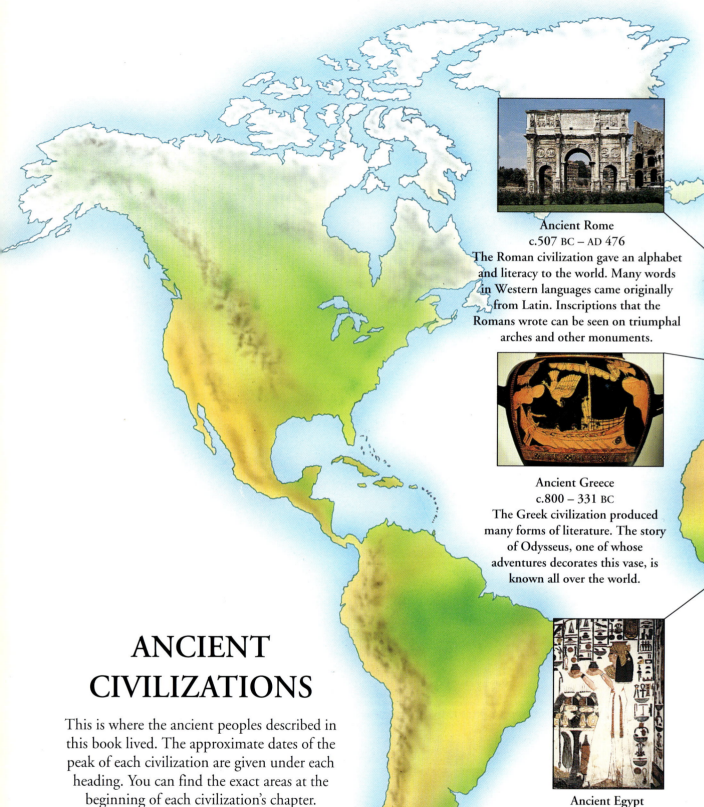

Ancient Rome
c.507 BC – AD 476
The Roman civilization gave an alphabet and literacy to the world. Many words in Western languages came originally from Latin. Inscriptions that the Romans wrote can be seen on triumphal arches and other monuments.

Ancient Greece
c.800 – 331 BC
The Greek civilization produced many forms of literature. The story of Odysseus, one of whose adventures decorates this vase, is known all over the world.

Ancient Egypt
c.3100 – 30 BC
The ancient Egyptians recorded facts about their daily lives on the exquisite wall-paintings that decorated their tombs. They also invented a new form of writing material, papyrus, from which we get the word 'paper'.

ANCIENT CIVILIZATIONS

This is where the ancient peoples described in this book lived. The approximate dates of the peak of each civilization are given under each heading. You can find the exact areas at the beginning of each civilization's chapter.

Ancient Phoenicia
c.1200 – 146 BC
The Phoenicians invented the phonetic alphabet
from which Greek and Latin alphabets were
derived. The Phoenicians were great traders, and
their influence extended all over the Mediterranean.

Ancient China
Ch'in dynasty c.221 – 206 BC
T'ang dynasty c.618 – 906
The ancient Chinese used seals,
like this one made of jade, to
give authenticity to important
documents. Their writing
system, like everything else,
developed in isolation from the
rest of the world. China has the
longest recorded history of
any ancient civilization.

Ancient Sumeria
c.3200 – 2300 BC
The Sumerians kept accounts and records by
drawing pictures on clay tablets. The pictures
developed into cuneiform, a writing system that
was later widely used throughout the Middle East.

Ancient Babylonia
c.1900 – 539 BC
Babylonian scribes sometimes used ivory
writing boards covered with wax as an
alternative to clay tablets. This one has a series
of astrological omens written in cuneiform.
Wax tablets were used for note-taking right up
until the end of the Roman Empire.

chapter one

WORDS:
MODERN AND ANCIENT

People have been speaking to each other for at least 100,000 years, but writing was only invented about 5,000 years ago. We use language to tell stories, sing songs, or just to chat. Words are funny when we tell a joke, informative when we learn, and they can be beautiful when we speak poetry. They are an essential part of daily life.

Language developed over thousands of years, from the first words used by Stone Age cave dwellers.

▲ *Writing began with simple pictures like these, which are engraved on stone. The stone is about 5,000 years old.*

▶ *The famous animal paintings in the caves at Lascaux, France. This Stone Age art came before writing, and its purpose is unknown.*

▶ *The letters used in today's Western alphabets are very nearly the same as the letters chiselled on this 1st century* AD *Roman tombstone. The tombstone belonged to a Greek called Longinus.*

Living and hunting food together they would be working as teams, and would learn how to warn each other of danger. To do this, they must have used recognizable sounds. These sounds later became the first words.

Before writing was invented, people had to remember everything. It was difficult to pass on accurate information even from one generation to the next. Writing is a way of storing information, and at first it consisted of stylized pictures of people, animals and everyday objects. People in many parts of the world, who spoke different languages, developed distinct ways of writing as their civilizations advanced. This book looks at some of them.

◄ *The buildings of Wukoki, an old Hopi word meaning Big House. Like the Basques in Europe, the Hopi have a language that developed independently of any other.*

New languages, such as the universal language Esperanto, were invented in the nineteenth century. The idea behind Esperanto was to create a language that any educated person could easily understand and use. Although Esperanto is still studied by a few people, it is rarely used today. People would rather speak their own language than a made-up one.

La floro en la vazo sur longa tablo estas ruga rozo.
The flower in the vase on the long table is a red rose.

▲ *All the words in Esperanto can be contained in a small dictionary.*

An entirely different form of writing, musical notation, is used by composers to write down the notes of musical tunes.

► *Making letters of the alphabet stand for musical notes started with the ancient Greeks, and the Romans had a similar system. Since the fourteenth century, in the West, musical notes have been written in much the same way. Lined music paper was invented much later. In Britain, Germany and the USA notes are called A, B, C, D, E, F and G. But in Italy and France, they are given names, ut, re, mi, etc.*

In 1829 the Frenchman Louis Braille invented a raised point form of writing that blind people could both read, using their fingertips, and write.

Because language can be written down, we can read today about the thoughts of people who lived nearly 5,000 years ago! However, although reading and writing are taught nearly all over the world, only one adult in two can write fluently.

▲ *A blind woman reading Braille. Many languages can be written in Braille.*

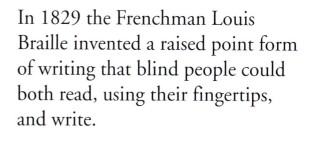

◄ *In the Pyrenees, between Spain and France, the people speak Basque. This language does not resemble any other and may have developed independently.*

As information technology grew in the twentieth century to become the biggest industry in the world, new languages that enable people to communicate with machines have been developed. One of these, called BASIC, or Beginners All purpose Symbolic Instruction Code, uses English-like words that can control how a computer operates.

▲ *Mini tape recorders are light and small, and as easy to carry as a pen and a pad of notepaper. They serve the same purpose – to make quick notes on the spot. The notes can be expanded and typed out later.*

chapter two

ANCIENT
SUMER

Today, the busy executive uses a Filofax or an electronic personal organizer to keep track of meetings, flight departures, the names of clients, telephone numbers and other vital information. In southern Mesopotamia, about 6,000 years ago, busy Sumerian farmers also found it difficult to remember details accurately. So they drew pictograms – little pictures of things such as ears of barley, or an ox's head – to stand for crops and animals. They also invented signs for numbers. Such farming records, scratched on wet clay tablets, are the very first evidence of when people began to write.

Then the Sumerians had a revolutionary idea. Why not use a pictogram to represent the sound of its name? For

People write in all directions. Arabic and Hebrew scripts are written from right to left. India has more than 800 languages and many scripts; some read from right to left, others from left to right. Chinese is written in symbols, from top to bottom and from right to left.

example, in English, a simple picture of a bee and a tray together could stand for the word 'betray', or a drawing of the sun could also be used to mean 'son'. Pictorial signs that represent sounds are called phonograms. Today's phonetic alphabets are their descendants.

▲ *Archaeologists digging in Mesopotamia found thousands of Sumerian clay tablets in the rubbish dumps they uncovered. This early administrative tablet, dating from about 2900 BC, lists areas of fields and crops. It reads from top right.*

In the West, words are written from left to right, using letters of the Roman alphabet. They are spelled with letters, and combinations of letters, that represent sounds. This is called phonetic spelling.

Now, we are all familiar with both kinds of signs. As people travel on holiday or on business, they are helped by easy-to-recognize signs, which are really modern pictograms. The signs for somewhere to eat (knife, fork, plate or cup) or a telephone (telephone handset), are used nearly everywhere.

◄ *A cylinder seal is like a small, round peg with a pattern carved on it. It was often made of ivory, or sometimes of semi-precious gems. The seal was rolled across wet clay to make an image. People have used seals since ancient times. A seal put on an object is a sign of ownership.*

► This advertisement is familiar to many people. Even if you do not know the language an advertisement is written in, you can often guess what it is about. This is because most well-known companies have an emblem, or sign, that everyone recognizes.

Throw-away ballpoint and fibre-tipped pens, printed with advertising slogans are often given out by companies. The advertisement usually contains writing and a sign – the company logo. It can be an object (a pictogram), or represent an idea (an ideogram). Now manufactured by the million, pens are very cheap. They and paper to write on are part of our everyday lives.

The Sumerians did not have paper, but they had plenty of clay. Gradually, they perfected a system of writing on damp clay, forming the clay into rectangular, postcard-sized tablets. At first, the Sumerians used a stick to draw pictures on them. Later, they developed a stylus cut into a wedge shape.

◄ What nineteenth century invention writes much faster than a pen? The first practical typewriter, invented in 1867. Modern societies need commercial schools to teach business skills. Some ancient societies had schools for the scribes who did official work.

When children learn to read, they learn the sound groups of letters make: they learn phonetically. The writing on this baked clay tablet is called cuneiform. There were many styles of cuneiform, since it was used for about 3,000 years and in many countries.

A stylus was usually made from tough reeds, sometimes from metal or bone. These were thrown away when the writing was finished.

In practice, the curved lines the Sumerians first made in pictograms were difficult to see after the clay tablets dried in the hot sun. So they made the lines straighter. Straight lines and wedge-like shapes were easier to press into wet clay and they did not change as the clay dried. Many tablets from around 3000 BC are filled with wedge-shaped writing. This writing is called cuneiform, from the Latin for wedge – *cuneus*. Cuneiform is the oldest known writing.

Clay writing tablets, unlike paper, last a very long time, which is why we know so much about the Sumerian civilization. Sumer flourished until it was conquered by the Babylonians in 1720 BC.

Many important records today are kept on magnetic discs or on microfilm. When a big new building is constructed, a time capsule that contains items of current interest is often buried in the foundations. Will a future archaeologist be able to decipher our records if they survive?

chapter three

ANCIENT
BABYLONIA

Planning a journey? Travel agents can give you a plan that shows you how to get from the airport to the hotel. Hiring a car? Car-hire firms often give out maps showing the quickest route out of town and how to get to set destinations. We are accustomed to an enormous choice of useful maps, plans and diagrams.

▼ *This Babylonian plan is the first that shows the whole world. It places Babylon on the Euphrates river, and shows the mountains of northern Assyria and the swamps to the south.*

If you live in the Britain, the maps in your school atlas begin with the British Isles, and the world map shows Europe clearly at the centre of the world. If you live in America, the atlas starts with the USA! The oldest map of the 'world' yet discovered was made by the Babylonians in about 700 BC. They did the same thing. Babylon, their main city, is placed right at the centre of the map and it is surrounded by water – probably the Mediterranean Sea.

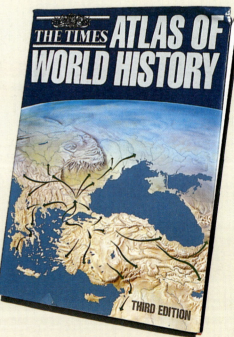

THE TIMES ATLAS OF WORLD HISTORY

THIRD EDITION

▲ *The cover illustration on this modern atlas shows an area similar to the ancient Babylonian plan.*

◄ *The most important library of the ancient world was at Alexandria in Egypt. It may have contained 700,000 papyrus volumes. A modern library contains thousands of printed books and computerized information.*

The Babylonians wrote textbooks in cuneiform on astronomy, law, science, mathematics, medicine, theology, magic and they even had dictionaries. Some 'books' were written on simple oblong clay tablets and others on many-sided clay cylinders. They were stored in special libraries, carefully indexed and arranged on shelves. The books in your local library are carefully indexed and arranged on the shelves according to subject. Each book is numbered with a code, called the Dewey Decimal System. This is an index that helps the librarian to keep track of all the books in the library.

◄ *Today letters are delivered to individual houses and offices, often twice a day.*

The next time you address an envelope, stick a stamp on it and put it in the nearest postbox, just think that your actions are very like those of some of the citizens in ancient Babylon. They were also able to send messages across the country by mail. It was King Cyrus the Great of Babylon who organized the first proper postal system in around 539 BC. Letters, written on clay tablets, were carried in clay envelopes along the 542 km of the King's postal route. The route crossed deserts from one oasis to the next and ran between 'posting' stations which connected the main cities of the Empire.

When Hammurabi, King of Babylon, conquered Sumer, the Babylonians adopted the Sumerians' cuneiform writing as well as their technique of writing on clay. The Babylonians improved the Sumerians' simple writing stylus to make styli of ivory, metal and glass.

Today, many businesses and private individuals write letters to each other without even using paper. Electronic mail, or E-mail, lets people use computers to send and receive letters across the world almost instantly, twenty-four hours a day.

◄ The Babylonian story of the flood, written on a clay tablet in about 700 BC, is just like the one in the Old Testament. Other tablets record military campaigns, religious feasts, and historical events.

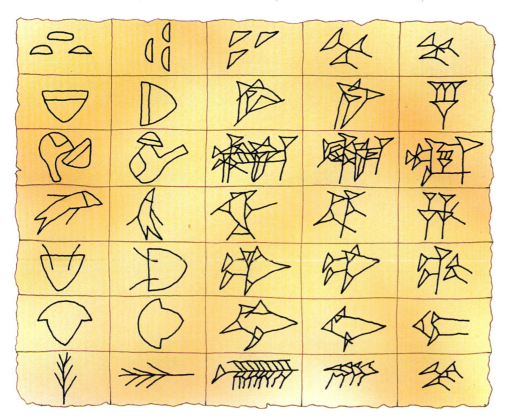

▲ This artwork shows how cuneiform developed from its original forms to the signs regularly used in Mesopotamia. The signs are for mountain, food, to eat, fish, ox, cow and barley/grain.

The cuneiform script, which has many hundred characters, could be used to write different languages in the same way the modern Latin or Roman alphabet can. Cuneiform writing spread to the surrounding countries of the Middle East, from Armenia in the north to Palestine in the south. At this time, other scripts were being invented, particularly in China and in Egypt.

chapter four

ANCIENT
EGYPT

We know a great deal about the ancient Egyptians because
they began to record their history as far back as 3100 BC.
In fact, they wrote on practically everything. With brush
pens made of rushes they marked papyrus, flakes of
limestone and pieces of wood. Papyrus scrolls, statues and
pyramids, as well as great quantities of art, were covered
with hieroglyphs, a form of Egyptian writing.

In ancient Egypt only boys went to school. Teachers believed that education could be beaten into their students. One of them threatens, 'With the hippopotamus whip I will teach your legs to idle around the streets.' Another declares, 'A boy's ears are on his back, he listens when he is beaten.'

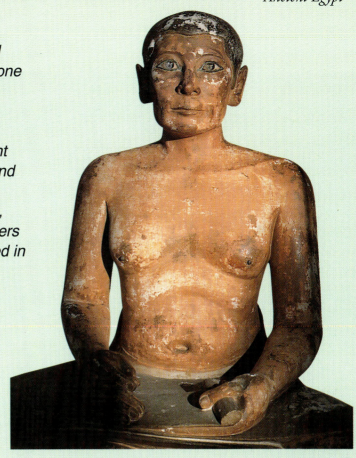

► *Scribes worked sitting down. This one is holding a roll of papyrus in his lap. Scribes were important in ancient Egyptian society and ranked with the priests, physicians, treasurers and others who lived or worked in the great temples.*

In ancient Egypt, everyone held scribes in such high esteem that they had special privileges: they were exempt from manual work and did not pay taxes. Today, in a similar way, the Irish government rewards artists and writers who come to live in Ireland with similar tax privileges. The Egyptians believed their god Thoth created writing as a gift to the world. The Greeks, impressed by the ancient Egyptian script, called it 'hieroglyphs' or sacred signs.

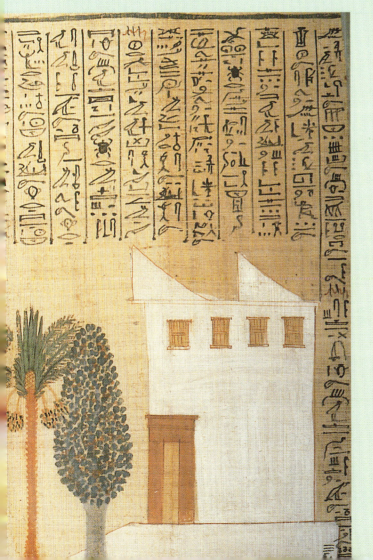

◄ *This picture is from the Book of the Dead, found in the tomb of Nakhte, an important scribe. The Book of the Dead tells the story of the journey of the souls of the dead to Osiris, the ruler of the Underworld. It is an illustrated guidebook to the afterlife, and a copy of the book was buried with anyone who could afford it.*

▼ A story can be told
simply and clearly
when pictures are
combined with words.
A cartoon strip is one
modern example.
Another example
might be a set of
illustrated instructions.

▲ The hieroglyphic
writing system was in
use for nearly 4,000
years. The Roman
alphabet, in which
most Western
languages are written,
has only been in use
for 2,000 years.
Hieroglyphic signs
face the beginning of
the line and are
normally read from
right to left. These
inscriptions on a
temple wall date from
about AD 140.

Very few strip cartoons have no words at all: pictures alone can be interpreted in different ways, so most have speech bubbles. The ancient Egyptians ran into the same problem of interpretation with their hieroglyphs, or picture writing. Like other ways of writing, Egyptian hieroglyphs began as pictograms – simple drawings of plants, flowers, birds and human figures. Pictograms, however, only stand for objects not ideas – two wavy lines could mean water, or possibly the sea or a lake. The ancient Egyptians sensibly put pictograms and ideograms together, to describe ideas as well as things. Two wavy lines stand for water but could also mean 'wet' or 'damp'.

Quite soon the Egyptians began using their script to represent the sounds of the Egyptian spoken language. Also, a flowing style of writing, like modern handwriting, was developed, later called hieratic. This was quicker to write than the combination of pictograms and ideograms.

Most modern road signs are ideograms. Because they are similar in many places around the world, they can be understood by drivers who cannot read a foreign language. Road signs are not the only ideograms we use today.

▲ A picture of a cigarette with a red line though it means 'do not smoke'.

▲ A little telephone in an address book means 'here is someone's phone number'.

▲ A picture of a man on a door does not mean 'this is a man', but 'in here is the men's room'.

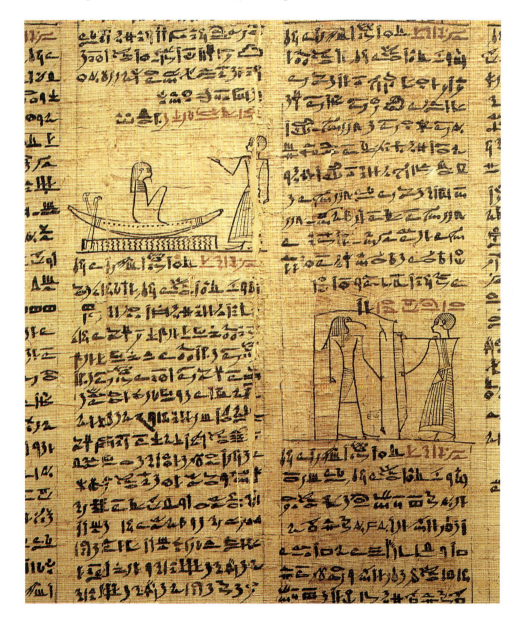

◄ *One way of writing fast is to use shorthand. Hieratic script is a shortened form of hieroglyphic writing. This sample comes from the Book of the Dead.*

▶ *The first hieroglyphic word made out on the Rosetta Stone was PTOLMYS. As the name of the king, it was always encircled. Then another encircled word was found with some of the same characters, P, L and O. It turned out to be KLIOPADRA. The three-language inscription on the Rosetta Stone is a decree passed by a council of Egyptian priests in 196 BC. The top band is Egyptian hieroglyphic writing. The bottom band is written in Greek and the middle band is in demotic Egyptian.*

In 1799, French soldiers digging the foundations of Fort St Julian, at Rosetta, near the mouth of the Nile, uncovered a slab of basalt, a dark stone. This chance discovery was the key to understanding Egyptian hieroglyphs. Now called the Rosetta Stone, the slab bears the same inscription in three different scripts: hieroglyphic Egyptian, Demotic (an easy-to-write version of hieratic) and Greek. The Frenchman

◀ *This early Egyptian calendar is written on papyrus.*

▼ *As the harvest is brought in, it is carefully measured and recorded by the seated scribes.*

Jean Francois Champollion, working from the Greek, made out the hieroglyphs in 1820. In 1821 the British captured the Rosetta Stone. It is now in the British Museum in London, England.

The ancient Egyptians farmed the fertile lands along the valley of the river Nile from around 4500 BC, and depended on the regular flooding of the river each year. The flooding spread silt on the land making it fertile: the farmers needed to know when this would happen, so an accurate calendar was devised. We still talk about months because the Egyptian calendar was based originally on the phases of the moon, which repeat twelve times a year.

Papyrus was the writing material of the ancient world. It was made from papyrus reeds grown in plantations in the Nile river valley. The papyrus-making industry was controlled by the state. The tall plants were harvested and the green rind removed from the stems. Thin strips cut from the white inner fibres were pressed together in overlapping layers. After drying in the sun, the papyrus was polished and rolled up into scrolls. Scribes wrote with a brush pen made from rushes. Curiously, in the nineteenth century, papyrus suddenly stopped growing along the banks of the Nile.

chapter five

ANCIENT
PHOENICIA

Trade, travel and immigration have always enriched language with new words. There are many words in English that come from faraway places. Cash, a Tamil word for a small coin; tea, a Chinese word; and pyjamas, khaki and bungalow, which all come from India, are just a few. When the Phoenicians set up trading posts, such as Carthage on the coast of Africa, they met people who used different writing systems. The Phoenicians built the first alphabet that used letters instead of cuneiform signs. They were among the first to write phonetically – a turning point in the story of writing. The Phoenicians' novel alphabet consisted of twenty-two consonants only, because, like other early alphabets, it left out the vowel sounds. The letter 'O', which the Phoenicians included in about 1300 BC, is the oldest unchanged letter of the alphabet.

▲ *Single letters of the alphabet are clearly seen in this Phoenician inscription. They are the direct ancestors of the letters used by the Greeks and the Romans.*

▶ *Two rows of oars propelled this swift Phoenician warship. It escorted the trading vessels that the Phoenicians sent throughout the Mediterranean. Phoenician glass products and trinkets have been found in Egypt and as far away as the Black Sea.*

Phonetics is the study of vocal sounds, the sounds that people make when they talk. In a phonetic alphabet the same letter or set of letters is always used to represent the same sound. A word is spelled out using groups of letters so that a reader knows how the word is pronounced.

The Phoenicians were sailors and the greatest traders of the ancient world. They lived along the coast of what is now Syria and Lebanon. The main Phoenician cities, Byblos, Sidon and Tyre, became powerful city states. Merchants from Byblos bought papyrus from Egypt and sold it to Greek traders. There are many modern words to do with books that come from the name Biblos, for example: bibliophile, bible, and bibliography.

▶ *Four gas turbines propel this giant airliner. It carries cargo all over the world in just a few hours. The language of aviation is English.*

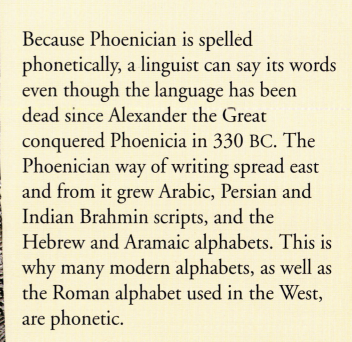

Because Phoenician is spelled phonetically, a linguist can say its words even though the language has been dead since Alexander the Great conquered Phoenicia in 330 BC. The Phoenician way of writing spread east and from it grew Arabic, Persian and Indian Brahmin scripts, and the Hebrew and Aramaic alphabets. This is why many modern alphabets, as well as the Roman alphabet used in the West, are phonetic.

chapter six

ANCIENT GREECE

We expect to see pictures of sporting and political events, natural disasters or even happy occasions whenever and wherever they happen. Throughout the twentieth century, many important events have been recorded on film. Now video cameras record everything, from the most important to the most trivial. When we want to know about any event, we can see pictures of it instantly, just because we have powerful recording techniques. But what if we were to lose our sophisticated technology?

► The Odyssey *tells of the adventures of Odysseus, making his way home after the war. Here, bound to the mast of his ship, he cannot succumb to the seductive voices of the sirens (sea nymphs).*

Something of the sort happened in ancient Greece.

An early Greek civilization, called Mycenaean after a town in southern Greece, was already highly advanced in 3000 BC. When it collapsed 2,000 years later, barbarian conquerors wiped out entire cities and destroyed the ancient culture. Reading and writing were forgotten, and Greece went through a 'dark age'.

▲ *A team of television cameramen video a football match so that millions of people around the world can watch it as it happens.*

Reciting a long narrative poem is an important way of keeping tradition alive when there is no writing or reading. Stories of mighty battles, heroic deeds and miraculous events in the Mycenaean world have survived from this time. They were later written down by Homer in his famous poems *Iliad* and *Odyssey*. At first thought to relate to mythical events, nineteenth and twentieth-century archaeology has revealed their historical truth.

The Iliad is the gripping first part of the story of the rescue of Helen, the beautiful wife of the King of Sparta, who had been kidnapped by the Trojans. (The Greeks eventually won the battle by hiding their soldiers inside a wooden horse, which the Trojans took inside their city.)

The Greeks played an extraordinary part in the story of language and writing. Hundreds of years after the barbarian invasions Greece rebuilt its lost civilization and culture, and Greek traders relearned the art of writing. Homer's poems and much else besides could now be written down. To begin with, the Greeks wrote in all directions, including in a spiral. In the ancient world, the Greek city of Alexandria had the most famous library, containing 700,000 rolls of papyrus. Euclid was among the many famous people who worked there. The Library of Congress in

One of the very old forms of Greek has been deciphered. Michael Ventris, an English architect, achieved this remarkable feat fifty years after the script, called Minoan Linear B, was found at the palace of Knossos on the island of Crete. Ventris had no Rosetta Stone, with two languages side by side, to help him. Instead, he used techniques more like cracking a modern military code.

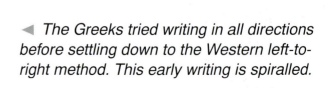

◄ *The Greeks tried writing in all directions before settling down to the Western left-to-right method. This early writing is spiralled.*

Washington DC, USA, contains about 100 million items, and nearly 1,000 km of shelves. Founded in 1800, it is the largest library of the modern world.

After 500 BC, the Greeks settled on writing from left to right. By then, they had perfected a complex writing system. The very first two Greek letters α (alpha) and β (beta) give us the word 'alphabet'. Both the Roman alphabet used in the West today, and the Russian Cyrillic alphabet, are descendants of ancient Greek.

▲ An amazing amount of evidence recounts the rebirth of Greek civilization. As well as inscriptions on coins, others were scratched on to pieces of unglazed pottery. There are accounts, lists of citizens, codes of law, and inscriptions on tombs.

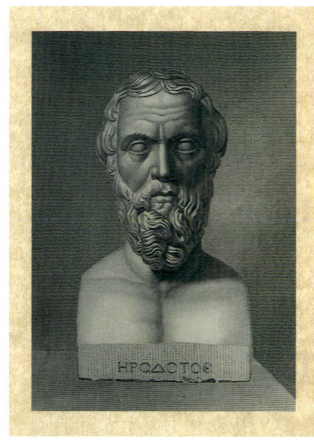

A Greek writer and historian called Herodotus, who lived in 500 BC, wrote detailed, action-packed accounts of the wars between Greece and Persia. In the very first history book, he described Phoenician voyages of exploration made in around 600 BC. Herodotus believed that the Greeks learned the art of writing from the Phoenicians, around 850 BC. They 'borrowed' the Phoenician alphabet and changed it to suit themselves mainly by adding letters for vowel sounds.

▲ *Here, at Epidaurus in Greece, is the best-preserved Greek theatre. In ancient Greece, drama competitions were held that lasted three days. Poets entered four plays each, three tragedies and a farce.*

Have you read a good novel recently or been to the theatre to see a comedy or a tragedy? The Greeks invented virtually all our forms of literature. From biography to oratory, to the dialogue spoken by the actors in dramas: it happened in Greece first. Even our words, comedy, tragedy, biography, oratory, dialogue, characters, dramatic, and lyric, come from the Greek. The writing of philosophers Plato and Aristotle, and playwrights Sophocles and Aristophanes

Thousands of surviving Greek manuscripts show us how parchment, vellum and other animal skins were used to write on. Scribes wrote with split-reed pens, used rulers to draw straight lines, and knives to make pens and to scrape out mistakes. For everyday note-taking, the Greeks used wax tablets with an iron or wooden stylus.

(noted for comedy), are a valued part of modern culture. Many of the plays are still performed regularly.

Each time there is an election, and people vote for the candidate of their choice, they are carrying on a method of government invented in the city state of Athens, Greece. Europe, the USA and many other parts of the world owe the gift of democracy to the ancient Greeks. The words democracy and politics come from ancient Greek. When 4,000 citizens of Athens scratched the name of a politician on pieces of broken pottery called 'ostraka', that politician was exiled from Athens, or ostracized.

Many words used today have their roots in ancient Greek:

grafo (write)- autograph, biography

mikros (small)- microphone, microscope, microbe

Arithmeo (number)- arithmetic

megas (large)- megabyte, megaphone, megawatt - and how about simply mega!

▲ *In South Africa, one of the newest democracies, citizens queue patiently to vote for the first time in their adult lives.*

chapter seven

ANCIENT
ROME

The calendar used in the West today is a legacy from ancient Rome because it is based on the calendar introduced by Julius Caesar in 46 BC. The ancient Egyptian calendar, in use for more than 4,000 years, assumed a year of 365 days. But this meant that every four years the calendar slipped behind the actual solar year by a full day. This error soon added up so the Emperor Julius Caesar adjusted the calendar by having a leap year every four years. The Julian calendar, as the new one was called, was used for over 1,500 years until it was changed again by Pope Gregory in 1582.

Turn back to page 29 of this book, and back again. Before the Romans invented the way books are bound, with separate pages, or leaves, sewn together and protected by a cover, you would have had to unroll a lengthy scroll of parchment or papyrus. Only one side of a scroll could be written on, and papyrus and parchment were expensive.

The West still uses the Gregorian calendar, but time is no longer measured by the rotation of the Earth, which is irregular. Instead an atomic clock, accurate to within 1 second every 300,000 years, sets the standard, and only very small adjustments are now needed. When in 1752 the last big adjustment happened in Britain, the people rioted, believing their lives had been shortened by eleven days.

▶ *Constantine was the first Christian emperor. He reversed the decline of the Roman Empire, which he ruled from the city of Constantinople. Constantine's Arch in Rome, like most Roman arches, has an inscription in Latin.*

In about AD 100, the Romans took sheets of parchment, folded and sewed them together. This was called a codex, and it is the ancestor of today's bound books.

The letters used to print the text of this book are technically called Roman. All Western languages are written with letters of the Roman alphabet. They have changed little in 2,000 years. As the Roman Empire grew by conquering land in Europe and around the Mediterranean, the Romans exported their language (Latin) their alphabet, their legal system, books and writing tools. Europe, and much of the rest of the world, owes the gift of literacy to the Romans.

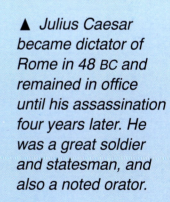

▲ *Julius Caesar became dictator of Rome in 48 BC and remained in office until his assassination four years later. He was a great soldier and statesman, and also a noted orator.*

Phoenician																										
𐤀 𐤁 𐤂 𐤃 𐤄 𐤅						𐤆 𐤇 𐤈 𐤉				𐤊 𐤋 𐤌 𐤍 𐤎 𐤏 𐤐 𐤑 𐤒 𐤓 𐤔 𐤕																

Classical Greek																										
A B Γ Δ E						Z H Θ I				K Λ M N Ξ O Π						P Σ T			Y		Φ X Ψ Ω		

Etruscan																										
𐌀 𐌁 𐌂 𐌃 𐌄 𐌅						𐌆 𐌇 𐌈 𐌉				𐌊 𐌋 𐌌 𐌍 𐌎 𐌏 𐌐 𐌑 𐌓 𐌔 𐌕																

Classical Roman																										
A	B	C	D	E	F	G		H		I		K	L	M	N		O	P		Q	R	S	T		V		X		Y	Z

Modern Roman																										
A	B	C	D	E	F	G		H		I	J	K	L	M	N		O	P		Q	R	S	T	U	V	W	X		Y	Z

▲ *The alphabet story starts with the Phoenicians. The Greeks learned to write again from the Phoenicians, after early Greek civilization was destroyed by invading barbarians. They improved the Phoenician alphabet by adapting it to their own language.*

The skilfully cut stone inscriptions made by the Romans were carefully planned beforehand. Before the letters and words were chiselled, chalk or charcoal sketches were made so that they were evenly spaced out. These Latin inscriptions can still be seen throughout Europe on fortifications and triumphal arches.

Just as Western countries owe their alphabet to the Romans, the Romans owed their knowledge of writing to the Etruscans, an ancient Italian civilization. The Etruscans had learned their alphabet from the ancient Greeks. By 300 BC, the Romans shaped the borrowed Greek and Etruscan scripts into a recognizable Latin alphabet.

The Romans valued education, and by the reign of the Emperor Augustus (63 BC to AD 14) most people could read and write. There were libraries of books which could be borrowed by anybody, including slaves.

Today magazines and books are produced electronically. In the days of ancient Rome, books were copied by hand and

◄ The tradition of beautiful writing, which has been important in many civilizations, was continued through the Middle Ages in brightly coloured, illuminated manuscripts.

▼ All Roman citizens were well-educated. Since they did not have paper or a cheap alternative, they wrote notes, as this girl is doing, on the smooth surface of a wax tablet.

the scribes who did the dull, day-to-day copying of books were often slaves. Then, the painstaking copying of manuscripts by hand, day after day, was exhausting work. 'It destroys your eyesight, bends your spine, squeezes your stomach and sides, pinches your lower back and makes your whole body ache,' wrote one fed-up scribe in a twelfth-century manuscript. It took many months for scribes to write out one book, so each book was a rare, precious possession that only the rich could afford. Today, the computer has replaced the scribes.

▶ *Battery-powered laptop computers are now as powerful as big desk-top computers. Because they can be used anywhere, business people can continue to work while travelling to conferences and meetings.*

Journalists, and sales and business executives who have to write on the move, depend on laptop computers. The Romans travelled extensively and invented ingenious unspillable ink pots to use when riding or on the march. They also had iron styli for writing on wax tablets, and quill pens made from goose feathers, and even metal pens, for use on papyrus and parchment.

Although Latin is no longer spoken, because European languages have many Latin words in them we can see similarities between one European language and another. About one third of the English language comes from Latin. Roman numerals are still used to describe kings and queens, for example Henry VIII (8th) of England, Louis XVI (16th) of France. They are also used on clockfaces and sometimes to give the year date: MCMXCV is 1995.

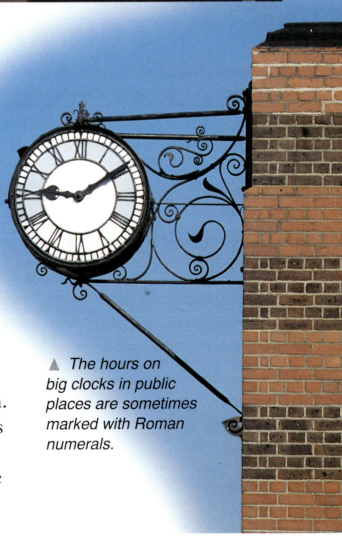

▲ *The hours on big clocks in public places are sometimes marked with Roman numerals.*

◀ *The New York city subway, in the USA has often been a target for modern graffiti artists.*

Latin phrases are still in common use, for example *status quo* (things as they are), *et cetera* (and the rest), *tempus fugit* (time flies) and *modus operandi* (the way it works). Birds and animals are classified into families in Latin. The Swedish scientist Linnaeus gave Latin names to plants, too. A dandelion is *taraxacum officinale*, and a buttercup, *ranunculus*. Drugs, largely made up from plants, still have Latin names.

▶ *The curse engraved on this Roman lead tablet reads: 'May he who carried Sylvia from me become as liquid as water.'*

People sometimes cannot resist putting graffiti on their urban surroundings. We may think such graffiti is a modern problem. However, the volcano Vesuvius erupted in Italy in AD 79 and buried the city of Pompeii in layers of deep ash. When archaelogists began to excavate the city in the nineteenth century, graffiti were found on the walls everywhere. Boasts: 'Celadus the Thracian . . . the answer to every girl's prayer.' Threats: 'Barca, you deserve to die!' Instructions: 'Don't foul the streets.' A drinker hopes the inn landlord will drown in his own bad beer. And someone writes, untruthfully, 'Everyone writes on the walls but me.'

chapter eight

ANCIENT CHINA

What has fortune telling got to do with the invention of writing? In ancient China, no important decision could be made without consulting the oracle bones. First deciphered in 1903, these animal bones and tortoise shells are inscribed with the earliest known Chinese writing. During the Shang dynasty of ancient China, priests prepared animal shoulder blades and shells by drilling holes in them. Then questions were written on them, and a very hot pointed piece of metal was pushed into the hole. The bones cracked and 'gave' answers to the questions. The priests made the answers permanent by writing with ink on the shell or bone.

The nomadic tribes that settled in China in about 2000 BC traded with the Sumerians and probably learned

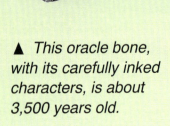

▲ *This oracle bone, with its carefully inked characters, is about 3,500 years old.*

written language from them. Chinese writing started with simple picture signs, but developed differently from Western alphabets. Chinese uses a mixture of pictograms, ideograms and signs and has separate characters for every word. This means a total of about 50,000 different signs. Chinese is spoken in different tones, which gives the same character several meanings. Fortunately, only about 3,000 characters are in everyday use, but all have to be memorized. There is one writing system for the many different languages and dialects spoken in China. This means that Chinese people who might not understand each other's spoken language can still read the same books and communicate in writing. Chinese signs and symbols were adapted in Japan, Korea, Vietnam and Mongolia.

English, spoken by about a third of a billion people, is the second most common language. It is the world language of science and business, and uses only twenty-six letters because it is written phonetically. But Mandarin, spoken by about three-quarters of a billion Chinese, is the most common native language in the world.

◄ *The Chinese are experts in making intricate carvings in jade, a semi-precious stone. Jade was a traditional material used to make seals. This imperial jade seal belonged to the Emperor Kuang-hsu.*

Chinese paper was a valuable export. For more than 600 years the technique of making it was a closely guarded secret. This knowledge spread to the world outside China when, in AD 751, Chinese prisoners were forced by their Arab captors to betray the secret. Paper-making in Europe began in the thirteenth century.

► Giant paper mills like this one turn trees into paper. The wood from one tree is sufficient for 400 copies of a 40-page tabloid newspaper. Trees used for papermaking may take 20-40 years to reach maturity, so it makes sense to recycle paper products.

When computers and word processors first arrived in offices, rash forecasts were made that the 'paperless' office had arrived. In fact, the world's paper consumption is so great that forests of trees are specially planted just for paper-making. Nearly all paper is now made from wood pulp. Paper-making machines produce a continuous sheet of paper 75 m wide at a rate of 900 m a minute.

◄ Paper making has changed little in over 2,000 years. Cellulose fibres obtained from pulped wood are made into a wet sheet of paper, which is then pressed and dried.

As information technology expanded in this century to become the greatest industry in the world, the strength of using a phonetic alphabet became clear. With less than thirty signs you can spell anything. This economy works well with computers. They depend on a way of coding letters and numbers called ASCII (American Scientific Code for Information Interchange), which gives a number to each character. ASCII cannot cope with Chinese and similar pictograms, ideograms and signs. This limitation, imposed by the standard QWERTY keyboard and ASCII, has so far restricted the use of computer techniques for Eastern languages like Chinese. The extraordinary growth in the number of fax machines enables people to send written information, including Chinese and Japanese electronically.

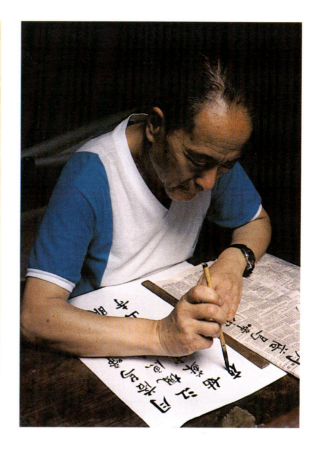

Cai Lun, a eunuch at the imperial court, is credited with the invention of paper in AD 105. While Europe was still using costly parchment, the Chinese became experts in the art of paper-making, using tree bark, old fishing nets and linen rags. This was very like the way in which we now make paper from recycled materials.

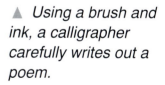
▲ Using a brush and ink, a calligrapher carefully writes out a poem.

◄ Chinese and Japanese typewriters have to use a very large number of characters. This makes the machine cumbersome and slow.

▶ *Old Chinese script is easy to read because of the changes the Grand Councillor of the First Emperor, Li Ssu, made to the way Chinese is written. Written Chinese was standardized for all future generations. This manuscript is thought to be an example of his writing.*

Because written Chinese has not changed much in more than 4,000 years, ancient texts can still be read. The shapes of Chinese symbols changed when different writing materials were used. Bamboo styli became popular for writing on silk, bamboo and wood. Ink was made in solid sticks, and like the Egyptians, the Chinese made it from lampblack, (which came from the oil burnt in their lamps), mixed with water and plant gums. Printing with carved wooden blocks on textiles and paper – an ancient Chinese art – was not developed in Europe until the fifteenth century. The Chinese used carved blocks of wood, ivory or stone, or seals cast in

The same idea sometimes turns up in two different places. In Germany, Johannes Gutenberg, without any knowledge of Chinese printing, invented the first mechanical printing press in 1447. It used moveable type. By the end of that century, a press printed as much in a day as a scribe could write in a year. Books became widely available to ordinary people for the first time. This made education possible for all and changed the culture of Europe. Radio and television in the twentieth century similarly made the control of information by repressive regimes more difficult.

bronze and by the seventh century AD they had invented moveable type, making separate pottery blocks to print each character. By AD 1086 the number of books printed began to overtake hand-painted manuscripts. The thoughts of the great philosopher Confucius, the poetry of Po Chu-yi, the work of artists Kuo Hsi and Fan K'uan, and of historians like the father-and-son team Ssu-ma Tan and Ssu-ma Ch'ien, were printed and available to all. The press was used all over China, while in Europe scribes were still copying out books by hand.

► *Painted Chinese writing became an art form in itself. A Chinese character is composed of up to twenty-six different brush strokes. But there are only five basic strokes which must be written in the correct order. This painting of a landscape in the rain uses ink and paint on paper.*

Ancient Greece and Crete

Before 3000 BC	2000 BC	1000 BC	0	AD

3000
●
Early Greek civilization writing in Minoan Linear A and B scripts.

1100
●
Greek lands conquered, ancient culture destroyed.

850
●
Greeks re-learn art of writing from Phoenicians.

730
●
From inscriptions on pottery, Greeks known to be writing again.

c.500
●
Greek historian Herodotus writes first known history book.

400–500
●
Heyday of Greek literature.

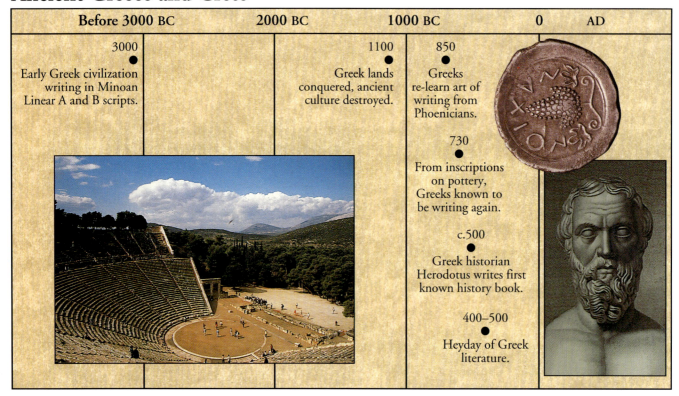

Ancient Rome

Before 3000 BC	2000 BC	1000 BC	0	AD

735
●
Legendary date of founding of Rome.

300–400
●
Rome developed Latin alphabet.

133
●
Rome had become a world power.

c.60
●
Most Romans can read and write.

46
●
Julius Caesar introduces Julian calendar.

100–200
●
Scrolls being replaced by the codex.

313
●
Rome adopts Christianity.

476
●
Roman Empire collapses.

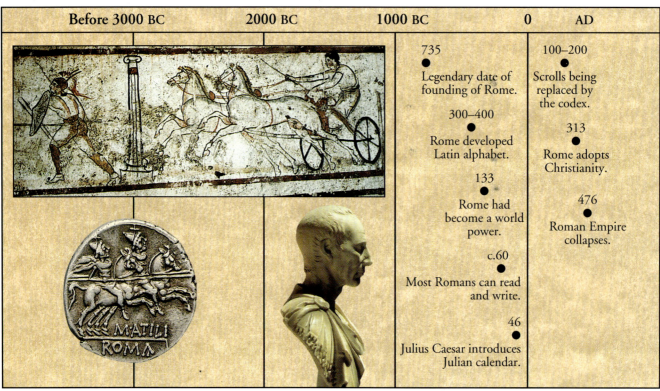

Ancient China

Before 3000 BC	2000 BC	1000 BC	0	AD

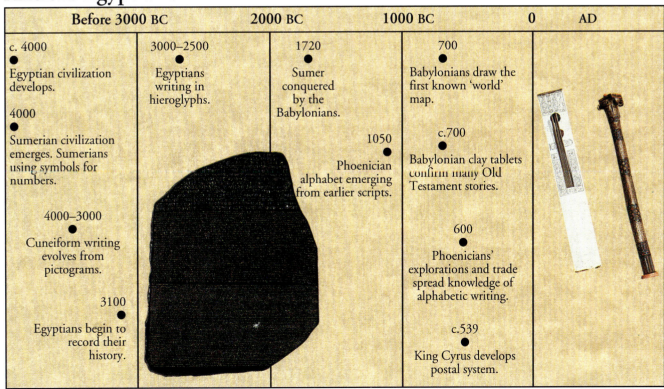

2000
Nomadic tribes settling around China; begin to trade with other nations.

1500
Chinese pictograms had progressed to ideograms.

1324–1266
Chinese writing in pictograms.

1000
Chinese printing on silk with carved blocks.

800
Inscribed boulders and bronze show that a true script had developed in China.

213
In China, Emperor Shih-huang-ti burns all books, draws up new list of characters.

100
Chinese invent paper.

600–700
China develops moveable type.

751
Secret of paper-making spreads westwards from China.

868
Chinese produce first printed book.

Ancient Egypt and the Middle East

Before 3000 BC	2000 BC	1000 BC	0	AD

c. 4000
Egyptian civilization develops.

4000
Sumerian civilization emerges. Sumerians using symbols for numbers.

4000–3000
Cuneiform writing evolves from pictograms.

3100
Egyptians begin to record their history.

3000–2500
Egyptians writing in hieroglyphs.

1720
Sumer conquered by the Babylonians.

1050
Phoenician alphabet emerging from earlier scripts.

700
Babylonians draw the first known 'world' map.

c.700
Babylonian clay tablets confirm many Old Testament stories.

600
Phoenicians' explorations and trade spread knowledge of alphabetic writing.

c.539
King Cyrus develops postal system.

GLOSSARY

Aboriginal   The first inhabitants of a country, particularly Australia.

Alphabet   A set of letters used in writing a language, such as the Roman alphabet.

Archaeologists   People who dig up and study ancient remains.

Artefacts   Thing made up from human workmanship; often from ancient times.

Barbarians   Uncivilized, often savage people.

Character   A written letter, or a symbol or other distinctive mark.

Colonized   Having settled in and developed another country.

Codex   Early form of book made by sewing sheets of parchment together, invented by the Romans.

Communicate   To give information to, and share feelings with, another person.

Communities   People living together in the same place.

Consonant   Any letter of the alphabet except a, e, i, o, and u.

Graffiti   Writing or drawing scratched, scribbled or sprayed on to a surface such as a wall.

Hieroglyphic   A picture of an object that represents a word, or a syllable or a sound used in ancient Egyptian writing.

Ideogram   A symbol that conveys the idea of a thing.

Leap year   A year with 366 days. It occurs every four years when February has twenty-nine days.

Literate   Able to read and write.

Literature   Writings such as poetry, plays and novels.

Papyrus   Early form of paper made from thin layers of reeds pressed together.

Parchment   Animal skin used for writing on, usually prepared from sheep or goats.

Phonetic   A system of spelling where there is a direct correspondence between the symbols used and the sound they represent.

Philosophy   Using argument or reason in the pursuit of wisdom and knowledge, or the study of the meaning of life.

Pictogram   A pictorial symbol for a word or phrase.

Scribe   A person, usually in medieval or ancient times, who copies documents.

Solar   Influenced by the sun.

Stone Age   A prehistoric period which started about 3,500,000 years ago when weapons and tools were made of stone.

Stylus   An early kind of pen with a sharp point at one end.

Translations   Books or documents that have been changed from one language to another.

Vowels   Any of the letters a, e, i, o, or u.

BOOKS TO READ

Signs and Symbols – Writing and Numbers by Jean Cooke (Wayland, 1990)

My First Library – Communication by Keith Wicks
  (Macdonald Educational, 1985)

Club 99 – Write Away by Viv Edwards (A & C Black, 1991)

My First Technology Library – Books by Diane McClymont (Macdonald, 1988)

Looking back at – Sending Messages by Anne Mountfield
  (Macmillan Educational, 1988)

Scripts of the World by Suzanne Bukiet (Mantra, 1989)

Kingfisher Classics – The Odyssey by Robin Lister (Kingfisher, 1987, 1990)

The Legend of Odysseus by Peter Connolly (Oxford University Press, 1986)

Calligraphy by Caroline Young (Usborne, 1990)

Picture acknowledgements:
The publishers would like to thank the following for allowing their pictures to be used in this book: Coca Cola Britain and Ireland 12 (top); Mary Evans Picture Library 15 (top); Robert Harding 4 (top), 6-7, 10-11, 13 (centre), 16 (top and centre), 27 (top), 28 (top), 32-3, 33, 37 (top), 38 (centre), 42, 44 (bottom left), 45 (bottom); Michael Holford 4 (centre), 5, 6 (centre), 11 (top) 14, 22, 23 (top and centre), 24 (centre and bottom), 25 (bottom), 26-7, 29 (top), 37 (centre) 38-9, 44 (top and bottom), 45 (right and bottom); Daniel Lodge 12 (top); J Rowe 10 (top), 12 (bottom), 14, 15, 20 (centre), 29 (bottom) 36 (top), 40 (centre), 44 (top left); Topham 4 (bottom), 31, 35 (top), 40 (bottom), 41 (top); Werner Forman Archive 18-19, 19, 20 (top), 21, 35 (bottom); Zefa 8.
The photo on page 15 (bottom) is courtesy of West Sussex Library Services.
All artwork is by Peter Bull.

INDEX

Numbers in **bold** refer to illustrations.